Strangers Among Us

by
Aaron Bushkowsky

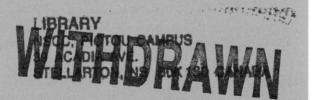
Playwrights Canada Press
Toronto Canada

Strangers Among Us © Copyright 1999 Aaron Bushkowsky
Playwrights Canada Press
54 Wolseley Street, 2nd Floor
Toronto, Ontario CANADA M5T 1A5
(416) 703-0201   fax (416) 703-0059
cdplays@interlog.com   http://www.puc.ca

Playwrights Canada Press acknowledges the support of The Canada Council for the Arts for our publishing programme and the Ontario Arts Council.

Cover design by Jodi Armstrong. Playwright photo by Nick Seiflow. Production shots by Glen Erikson Photo.

Canadian Cataloguing in Publication Data

Bushkowsky, Aaron, 1957
    Strangers among us

A play.
ISBN 0-88754-584-X

1.Title.

PS8553.U69656S77 1999   C812'.54   C99-932597-3
PR9199.3.B87S77 1999
Printed and bound by Hignell Printing
at Winnipeg, Manitoba, Canada.

Through the ages, theatre has been an excellent vehicle for telling complicated, powerful and emotional stories. Alzheimer's disease is all that, because it attacks the very thing that makes us human – our mind.

As a research-based pharmaceutical company, the work of Pfizer is based on the power of the mind. That, and our success in bringing to Canadians the first medication to treat symptoms of mild to moderate Alzheimer's disease, made our involvement with *Strangers Among Us* a natural.

Pfizer Canada was proud to sponsor the play's premiere presentation at Vancouver's Roundhouse Theatre in October, 1998 and is thrilled to be the title sponsor of its national tour across Canada. We cannot think of a more appropriate way to mark the millennium than to face up to one of the great challenges of our time – overcoming Alzheimer's disease.

This book is dedicated to all senior artists who continue to create, perform and work in the arts, and to my wife, Katey, whom I plan to become an older artist with.

Aaron Bushkowsky has been produced and published in several genres. His book of poetry *ed and mabel go to the moon* was nominated for the Dorothy Livesay Award for Best Book of Poetry in BC. His short stories have been published across Canada. His short film "The Alley" aired on CBC, won the National Screen Institute drama prize, was nominated for six Leos (BC Film Awards) and was invited to screen at the Siena Short Film Festival in Italy. His plays, which include the award-winning *Strangers Among Us*, have been produced throughout Canada. Aaron has served as playwright-in-residence at Touchstone Theatre in Vancouver and as a resident film-writer at the prestigious Canadian Film Centre in Toronto. He writes in Vancouver, BC, where he resides with his wife, actress Katey Wright, three cats and a dog.

ACKNOWLEDGMENTS

The playwright wishes to acknowledge the wonderful guidance and assistance of Joy Coghill, founding Artistic Director of Western Gold Theatre, and Thor Arngrim, producer, who are responsible for the idea of writing a play about Alzheimer's disease for a group of senior artists. Thor passionately believed in the play and the national tour, and has worked tirelessly to make it all happen. His vision of hope for Alzheimer's disease will touch many. The playwright also acknowledges the financial assistance of Western Gold Theatre through a commission for writing *Strangers Among Us*. A special thanks to Pfizer Canada Inc., whose commitment to this play made everything possible. And finally, thanks to Bunny Wright for the title *Strangers Among Us*.

Strangers Among Us was commissioned by Western Gold Theatre, and was originally staged at the Roundhouse Theatre, Vancouver, B.C., October 15-31, 1998.

NETTY, MARY 2	Susan Chapple
GABRIELLE	Doris Chillcott
ART	Craig Davidson
ROBYN	Barbara McColl
LEO	Barney O'Sullivan
MARY, JOAN	Sheila Paterson
MICHAEL	Grant Reddick
VIRGIL	Lee Taylor

WESTERN GOLD THEATRE SOCIETY

Joy Coghill, C.M.	Artistic Director
Director	Kathleen Weiss
Producer	Thor Arngrim
Associate Producer	Daphne Goldrick
Choreography	Susan McKenzie
Set and Costume Design	David Owen Lucas
Lighting Design	Gerald King
Sound Design	Jeff Corness
	with Ted Hamilton
Dramaturge	Pamela Hawthorn
Properties	Erinne Drake
Wardrobe	Taryn O'Gorman
Stage Manager	Todd Bricker
Apprentice Stage Manager	Bev Walker
Production Manager	James Pollard

This play was nominated for four 1999 Jessie Theatre Awards (Outstanding Lead Actor, Outstanding Lead Actress, Outstanding Production and Outstanding Original Script). It received a Jessie for Outstanding Original Script. Western Gold also received a Jessie for Outstanding Community Contribution.

CHARACTERS

JOAN	(Michael's daughter),	50
ART	(Joan's husband),	55
MICHAEL	(has Alzheimer's),	70s
GABRIELLE	(has Alzheimer's),	70s
VIRGIL	(Gabrielle's husband),	70s
NETTY	(Gabrielle's daughter),	30s
ROBYN HOPKINS	(a nurse),	40s or 50s
LEO	(baseball player),	70s

CHORUS

MARY	(cake),	60s
MARY 2	(dancing),	60s

Other Alzheimer's patients

SET

Perhaps boxes with poles sticking out of them. On the poles, sails where images can be projected. In between scenes, actors can sit behind the boxes as if sitting in sailboats. The sailboats are moveable with one side white.

NOTES

The play is dreamy and non-linear. As the play continues the main part of the chorus (LEO, MARY and MARY 2) wear more and more colourful clothing so their bodies become works of art.

The scenes can flow into each other quickly. Projections are optional. The play can be performed by 7-10 actors with doubling of the roles.

ACT ONE

Scene One

Lights up. Eerily silent. A row of sails.

The actors enter wearing grey overcoats. They appear lost and wander around trying to make sense of their surroundings and each other. Among them are GABRIELLE, wearing a fancy coat and MICHAEL, wearing a long coat.

Suddenly appearing: a host of lights coming from the windows of houses from across the shore (in Vancouver — the lights of North Vancouver). Everyone is drawn to the lights. They reach for them, then slowly exit.

MICHAEL and GABRIELLE remain. They make their way to a bench at a bus stop.

GABRIELLE   *(to MICHAEL)* Could you...? *(she laughs)* Have you ever been to the North Shore?

MICHAEL   Don't like California, except for the wine.

GABRIELLE   No... no, across the bridge?

MICHAEL   My father was an engineer.
Worked on roads.
The occasional bridge too.
A good man but a mean temper.
Liked to drink.
Spirits.

GABRIELLE   *(showing MICHAEL a note)* Do you know where this is? Please...

MICHAEL You should try to improve your penman-
ship.

GABRIELLE *(more agitated)* Do you know where I am?

MICHAEL I certainly do.

GABRIELLE My husband will think I'm nuts if I don't
show up.

MICHAEL My children... I moved in with them.
Now they ask me things I can't answer.

GABRIELLE I really must go home, can't keep Virgil
waiting.

MICHAEL I have a cousin named Virgil.
Lost his thumb during the war.
That's before they started sewing things
back on.

GABRIELLE I should have worn a sweater tonight...
I have this beautiful sweater.

MICHAEL Sweaters are very comfortable.

GABRIELLE Kathryn bought it for me in London.
My sister's very generous with her money.
Pounds I should say, more correctly.

MICHAEL London was the name of my dog...
Remember that show?
That show with the dogs...

GABRIELLE I never go to the theatre.

MICHAEL Theatre?

GABRIELLE Theatre.

MICHAEL *(pause)* Yes well... lights, lights, lights. All
those lights... you wonder how they
remember.

GABRIELLE   I just left the house for a moment.
Wanted to look at Ellie's roses...
Just down the street.

MICHAEL   You know, the cabs in this city are very
dirty.

GABRIELLE   I should have told someone.
But... twenty years I've lived here.
Twenty years. I should know.

MICHAEL   Ah... I don't know what's going on.
This guy, this cabby
He drove like a Russian.
A mad Russian.

GABRIELLE   Babushka.

MICHAEL   This guy. Mr. Big Shot.

GABRIELLE   Babushka.

MICHAEL   One of those thin cigars... I'm sure of it.
Stinks the whole place up.

GABRIELLE   A neighbour we called Babushka.
Smoked like a chimney.
But beautiful tomatoes in her yard.

MICHAEL   Some cabby alright.
Dropped me here.
The main route... what a joke.

GABRIELLE   Somebody will come for us, right?

MICHAEL   Oh yes. Young people I hope.
(beat) My grandkids love their chips and
Coke, chips and Coke. When I was their
age we ate wheat.
Rubbed the husks right in our hands.
You have thin hands.
You must have rheumatism.

GABRIELLE   No, my father.
Me? I have my own problems.

MICHAEL   Yeah... well, at our age...
(beat) Have you seen a bus?

GABRIELLE   No. *(beat)* Will they come for us soon?

MICHAEL   Well as long as it's not a motorcycle.
Terrible things.
And you have no protection.
None at all!

GABRIELLE   I'm cold.

MICHAEL   Give me your hand. *(she does)*
You should know better.

GABRIELLE   Yes I know. *(beat)*
I'm scared.

MICHAEL   It's alright. I'm right here.

GABRIELLE   Who are you?

MICHAEL   Michael. Named after an angel.

GABRIELLE   *(pulling back)* Weirdo.

MICHAEL   No, no.... Michael. He's in the Bible.
You really should know better.

GABRIELLE   *(beat)* What time is it?

MICHAEL   It's late.

GABRIELLE   Yes I suppose. Everybody sleeping.

MICHAEL   The whole works.

GABRIELLE   Every last one of them. Sleeping.

> *A moment. Car headlights suddenly illu-*
> *minate them, they look hopeful. But the*
> *car and the lights pass. A moment.*

MICHAEL "Past the near meadows, over the still
stream
Up the hill-side and now 'tis buried deep
In the next valley-glades:
Was it a vision, or a waking dream?
Fled is that music — do I wake or sleep?"

(beat) Well I wonder where the hell that
came from?

GABRIELLE It was beautiful.

MICHAEL I don't mean to lecture you.
But back then, that's what I did.

GABRIELLE Well those were the days.

MICHAEL Days of wonder.
Nights of sheer exhaustion.
Work, work, work...
Then out like a light.
Now look at me.

GABRIELLE *(taking his hand again and pausing)*
Myself.
I don't like to sleep anymore.

MICHAEL Me neither.

> *Lights fade. Images of houses projected.*
> *One house looks exactly like the next one.*

ACT ONE
Scene Two

Projected: "One must wait until the evening to see how splendid the day has been."

— Sophocles

It fades.

Two waiting rooms at a care facility. VIRGIL and NETTY, dressed conservatively in dull colours, are with GABRIELLE on one side of the stage while JOAN and ART, also dressed conservatively in dull colours, are with MICHAEL on the other. The action seems heightened. GABRIELLE and MICHAEL wear big coats and at least one piece of clothing that is of a bright colour.

Focus on MICHAEL, JOAN and ART.

JOAN   *(to MICHAEL)* You could have been killed out there.

MICHAEL   What?

ART   We were worried sick about you.

MICHAEL   You worry too much, keep it up and your hair will fall out.

ART   It already has.

MICHAEL   Quick... wrap your head in a towel soaked in linseed oil!

               Focus on VIRGIL, GABRIELLE AND NETTY.

VIRGIL   What happened to that note I gave you?

GABRIELLE   Note?

VIRGIL   I wrote our address down. In case of an emergency? You were supposed to show it to someone?

GABRIELLE   Who?

NETTY   Someone in authority, mom.

> *VIRGIL tries to take off GABRIELLE's coat.*

VIRGIL   ...and you end up with some crazy old man on the East Side!

GABRIELLE   No... I live on the North Shore. And my husband... sure he's a little crazy but I still love him.

VIRGIL   Oh God... *(looking around)* Does *anybody* work here?

GABRIELLE   Where are we anyway?

NETTY   At a facility.

GABRIELLE   What's that?

NETTY   It's a special place where they care for you.

GABRIELLE   And they get paid for that?

NETTY   Yes.

VIRGIL   Where is the nurse?

GABRIELLE   Why does your father want a nurse?

NETTY   Because he loves you.

GABRIELLE   That's a good one.

NETTY   I love you too, mom. *(she kisses GABRIELLE)*

GABRIELLE   Careful, it smears. Sometimes you put it on too thick.

> *Up again on MICHAEL, JOAN and ART.*

JOAN   The police said they found you on the East Side. How in the world did you end up there?

MICHAEL   I like to walk.

JOAN   We can't... I can't live this way, worried sick that they won't find you. This is the third time in a month. You weren't supposed to leave the yard!

MICHAEL   Look, I'm not asking you to do anything.

JOAN   You're driving me nuts!

MICHAEL   Watch your mouth. I'm still your father, Rachael.

JOAN   Joan. I'm Joan, father.

MICHAEL   Don't remind me, alright?

JOAN   Well get it right.

MICHAEL   I'm not stupid!

JOAN   Do we have to fight?

MICHAEL   I'm your father!

ART   Joan...

JOAN   Don't you Joan me.

MICHAEL pinches her bottom. JOAN jumps and slaps MICHAEL's hand.

JOAN Don't pinch! *(to ART)* Christ, he's always pinching me.

ART I pinch you, we all pinch you. We're crazy about you. Have a heart.

MICHAEL Rachael, born just after the war, had a little hole in her heart. And that was the beginning of the end I tell you. Makes me sad.

Up on VIRGIL, GABRIELLE AND NETTY.

VIRGIL I am your husband, Gabby. I love you and you love me and we'll see this thing through. You understand? *Understand!?*

GABRIELLE Why are you so upset?

VIRGIL You left the house, doors wide open and the burners were on high. The place could have gone up in smoke.

GABRIELLE *(embarrassed)* Oh my... when I was a teacher I was very organized.

VIRGIL Where is that nurse?

GABRIELLE You are not having a nurse!

NETTY Are you okay, mother?

GABRIELLE Not really. I wish I could go back to work.

NETTY Retirement doesn't suit you, does it?

GABRIELLE Is that what this is?

NETTY   You know, I still have all your learning aids.

GABRIELLE What are you talking about?

NETTY   Never mind.

GABRIELLE You're sure a big girl now.
Say "hi" to your mother for me when you see her.

NETTY   You are my mother.

GABRIELLE Well, say "hi" to her anyway.

NETTY   I will.

> *NETTY, VIRGIL, JOAN and ART fade into the background.*
>
> *A moment. GABRIELLE and MICHAEL are alone.*

GABRIELLE Where are we?

MICHAEL   Some kind of castle.

GABRIELLE No, no... the ceilings are too low.

MICHAEL   Some kind of holding area maybe.

GABRIELLE Why hold us? We didn't do anything.

MICHAEL   Well maybe they want to study us.

GABRIELLE Oh I don't think so.
My father always told me I was a very ordinary girl.

MICHAEL   We're stripes on a different tiger.

GABRIELLE   Speak for yourself.
            I am as human as human can be.
            I cry and laugh and do all that stuff in
            between.
            Human. Just human.

MICHAEL   I have this feeling in my chest.
            An animal clawing to get out.

GABRIELLE   You should get that looked at. Seriously.

MICHAEL   *(beat)* I like your hair.

GABRIELLE   I like your eyes.
            For an animal.

MICHAEL   *(an unsure moment, then softening)* You're
            something alright.

            Lights fade.

ACT ONE
Scene Three

*The other actors slowly enter. All are
dressed in overcoats.*

*Dreamy music swells. We are in the world
of Alzheimer's at the care facility. It may
feel like a country fair atmosphere.*

*LEO, MARY, and MARY 2 (who will act
as the main part of the chorus) remove
their overcoats. They are dressed in colourful eccentric clothes. They move toward
GABRIELLE and MICHAEL. They study
them carefully.*

*Projection: "A human being is part of the
whole, called by us the 'universe,' a part
limited in time and space."*
                                    — Albert Einstein

Enter ROBYN. She's the nurse.

MICHAEL Excuse me, who's in charge?

ROBYN I am.

MICHAEL What is it we've done, why are we here?

ROBYN It's because of what you've got that you're
here.

MICHAEL And what's that?

ROBYN A constant horrible sinking feeling, memo-
ries piling up behind like boxcars, no
engine to pull them anywhere.
Purgatory... basically.

Enter other Alzheimer's patients.

ROBYN   I'm sorry it's gone this far. But since we're
               here, we might as well have some fun.
               Look, everybody. We have some new peo-
               ple here today. Gabby and Michael. Why
               don't you introduce yourselves to them.

LEO   Played Double-A when I was young.
               A good ballplayer I was.
               Could turn a double-play like quicksilver.

ROBYN   Show us.

LEO   *(he pretends to catch or pitch)* I'm Leo
               Robinson. When I was 19 the world was
               my peach.

GABRIELLE   You were very lucky. I couldn't wait to
               get out of my teens.

LEO   *(he roars like a lion at GABRIELLE and
               MICHAEL)* I'm a dragon. Played a little
               ball up in Regina... you know... with the
               dragons. And oh yeah the scouts used to
               come up there in their three piece suits
               and big black boots, hit two dingers off
               Georgie White one afternoon.

MICHAEL   I never enjoyed sports.
               After you've dodged bullets, the rest of
               them pale in comparison.

LEO   What kind of game is that?

MICHAEL   Oh I don't think you'd understand.

LEO   You making fun of me?

MICHAEL   No.

LEO   You think I'm crazy?

MICHAEL   Of course not.

LEO	Good. *(beat)* Never married, myself. How 'bout you?
MICHAEL	Yes. A wonderful woman. But mind your own business.
MARY	Mary.
MICHAEL	Pleased to meet you.
MARY	I made a huge wedding cake in 1944. Can't stand the stuff myself, But just because I don't eat sweets doesn't mean I'm not.
MICHAEL	Do you read?
MARY	Of course. If you can't read... you can't write.
MICHAEL	Who are these people?
ROBYN	We all stay here at the facility. Together.
MICHAEL	And who are you?
ROBYN	Robyn.
MICHAEL	You don't look like a Robyn.
LEO	Look buddy, she's a Robyn, alright?
MICHAEL	*(to ROBYN)* What's your purpose here?
ROBYN	I'm here to help you.
MICHAEL	I'm not a cripple.
ROBYN	We all help each other.
MICHAEL	Oh... this is getting worse by the minute.

MARY   I learned to dance after my father died of
              euphemisms.
              A short man with sticky legs.
              In the end he couldn't quite catch his
              breath.

MICHAEL   *(to ROBYN)* I can't stay here, I'm sorry.

ROBYN   Do you know where we are?

MICHAEL   What's that supposed to mean?

ROBYN   Do you know where we are?

MICHAEL   I am an educated man...
              I know what's happening here!

ROBYN   You can't leave. I'm sorry.

MICHAEL   So I'm stuck...?

ROBYN   Well, in a way.

MICHAEL   Horrible situation... horrible.

MARY 2   It's okay... think on the bright side.

MICHAEL   You must be joking.

MARY 2   It's nice to meet you. I'm Mary too.

MICHAEL   Is anybody not Mary?

GABRIELLE   I'm Gabrielle.

MICHAEL   Yes.... you look familiar.

ROBYN   That's right, you two took a little walk last
              night... how did you find each other any-
              way?

MICHAEL   I don't know. Now, can I go?

ROBYN   What, and miss the dance?

> *Waltzing music up. LEO drifts up to*
> *MARY 2.*

LEO   Dance?

MARY 2   Thank you.

> *They waltz. MARY and ROBYN dance as*
> *well. MICHAEL and GABRIELLE sit*
> *watching the others dance.*

MICHAEL   I think we're stuck with a bunch of queer
ducks.

GABRIELLE   They're good dancers though.

MICHAEL   They're dancing and we sit here rotting
away.

GABRIELLE   Didn't you ever have a little fun?

MICHAEL   Had a ball at a bash just before I did my
duty.

GABRIELLE   We used newspapers.
Tore them up and stacked them beside the
toilet.

MICHAEL   No, no... what are you thinking?
I'm talking about Korea. All mud and
more mud.
Sticky rice and rubbery beef.
Roofs that always leaked.
Guns everywhere.

GABRIELLE   We just had to make do with what we
had.
Plum and apple jam. Used tea bags.
Old towels into rags.

MICHAEL Sure.
You just have to make do.
That's life.

GABRIELLE Like my father always said,
We all gotta turn our toes up some time.

LEO drifts up with MARY 2.

LEO You two gonna sit there all day like
bumps on a board?

MICHAEL Boards don't have bumps.
They're called knots.

LEO You think I'm crazy? Is that what you
think?

MARY 2 *(defusing LEO)* Come on, let's keep dancing.

LEO That boy's gonna be nothin' but trouble.

*A moment. MICHAEL notices
GABRIELLE rubbing her feet.*

MICHAEL You have small feet for a woman your age.

GABRIELLE Thank you.

MICHAEL Allow me, madame. *(taking one of her feet
and examining it)* They say the feet are
always connected to our souls.

GABRIELLE I have bad soles.

MICHAEL You have a fine soul but a bad arch.
Rub here and it's your kidneys.

GABRIELLE Do I know you? Or do you have a foot
fetish?

MICHAEL   Michael. Remember?
           And you really should know better.

GABRIELLE Yes. Of course. Michael. But what will
           my husband say? *(rubbing her foot hard)*
           Ow!

MICHAEL   Your heart.

GABRIELLE Oh my...

           *GABRIELLE pulls her foot away. They
           both sit there and watch the others exit. A
           moment.*

MICHAEL   I'm an educated man.
           Call me an academic.

GABRIELLE I would but I can't seem to find one any-
           where.

           They look at each other, then smile a bit.

MICHAEL   That's a good one. Very funny.

GABRIELLE Just lucky.

MICHAEL   Yeah, both of us. Just lucky, I guess.

           Lights fade.

MICHAEL
(Grant
Reddick) and
GABRIELLE
(Doris
Chillcott):
"You really
should know
better".

ACT ONE
Scene Four

*Lights up on VIRGIL and NETTY. They
watch MICHAEL and GABRIELLE who
are nearby sitting on chairs at the care
facility.*

VIRGIL Did I ever tell you she got a hole in one
once? On a green surrounded by water.
Up in the mountains. She had a beautiful
swing. Nice tempo. Kept her head down.
Great concentration. Good follow-
through. The ball landed soft like a cat on
a green as lush as your carpet. It took two
bounces and rolled into the cup. I turned
to her and said...
Well, she learned fast.

NETTY She's still got such beautiful eyes, doesn't
she?

VIRGIL Yeah I suppose.

NETTY You suppose?

*They watch GABRIELLE as she shuffles
along.*

NETTY Hi mom. We're here.

*GABRIELLE stops, then continues shuf-
fling away.*

NETTY (beat) You know I read somewhere the
other night that young lovers look exactly
alike to each other their whole lives. It's
everyone else that changes.

VIRGIL You read that in one of those ladies' maga-
zines?

NETTY   American Psychology.

VIRGIL   Strange name for a ladies' magazine.

NETTY   *(trying again)* What does mother look like
           to you, dad?

VIRGIL   *(not really looking)* Well. I don't know.

NETTY   Look.

VIRGIL   *(after a bit, he looks, then looks away)* You
           know, the other night I dreamt we were
           still all young and exotic. We were always
           in a hurry, always moving... to get to the
           next fancy dinner, the next business meet-
           ing, or to school to pick up the kids, what-
           ever. Now look at us. Half the time we're
           hunched over, walking around like we're
           looking for nickels. Plus I only eat three
           food groups: chicken, potatoes and prune
           juice. At night my stomach sounds like a
           gravel factory. And in the morning I eat
           breakfast on the toilet. It comes in a can.
           Some life, eh? *(laughing a little at his own
           joke)* You know, it wouldn't hurt you to
           laugh a little.

NETTY   Well dad, this is one of those times I just
           can't laugh.

VIRGIL   Oh you're going to get old before your
           time, I know it. Lemme give you some
           advice. Spend your money on clothes and
           trips and big fancy meals. You hear of an
           eclipse in South America. Go see it. Have
           some fun. Maybe you'll meet someone.
           Do it now and do it often because, you
           know, life is wink of an eye.

NETTY   Well, I have a son at home, I work part-
           time and I take care of my mother. But
           thanks for the advice.

>*A moment. GABRIELLE shuffles toward them.*

NETTY Hi mom. Look who's here. Dad.

>*GABRIELLE looks, then shuffles away.*

VIRGIL This is hopeless.

NETTY Look, just be here occasionally. Hold her hand, talk or walk with her. There's a golf course nearby. You can watch them hit balls.

VIRGIL I don't know.

NETTY You look at her over there. Look. That's your wife. The person you walked down the aisle with. The woman who laughed at all your jokes, who put up with your bad habits and visited every day when *you* were in the hospital. The same woman you whisked away to Montserrat for your first big romance. The same one you cradled in your arms, with the same face and hair and eyes. Come on dad. Go to her. Reassure her. It's okay.

>*A long moment. VIRGIL looks at GABRIELLE, then at his feet.*

VIRGIL I'm going to find a fountain. I'm sorry. I... I feel a little dry.

>*VIRGIL leaves.*

>*Lights fade as NETTY goes to comfort GABRIELLE.*

ACT ONE
Scene Five

Lights up on JOAN and ART trying to follow ROBYN, now dressed in a smock or overcoat again, as she walks with LEO and MARY 2. They are walking in circles at the care facility.

JOAN   I mean you *do* serve organic food here, don't you?

ROBYN   Nineteen fifty-nine... a good meal was steak and potatoes, lots of gravy and frozen peas that go moosh under your fork.

JOAN   What the hell is she saying, Art?

ART   I don't know but I'm hungry.

MARY 2 waltzes around him quickly.

JOAN   What kind of place is this anyway?

ROBYN   It's a place where they feel safe. We've developed our system to respond to their needs.

JOAN   They don't know what they need. If they did, they wouldn't be here.

MARY 2   *(to ART)* Do you know why they invented time?

ART   Why?

MARY 2   So everything doesn't happen all at once.

JOAN   Art, get involved a little here. Ask if they have a crafts program.

ART	What?
JOAN	Programs to keep them busy. Ask her.
ART	*(to MARY 2)* So you have programs here?
MARY 2	Oh yeah.
JOAN	Not her. Her!
ART	Oh. *(to ROBYN)* So... what kind of things do people do in here anyway?
ROBYN	Time travel mainly.
JOAN	What?
ROBYN	It's true.
JOAN	This is ridiculous. Where's my father?
ROBYN	Checking the plumbing.
JOAN	Plumbing? He hasn't done plumbing since before Korea.
ROBYN	He can still check, can't he?
JOAN	But he can't *do* anything.
ART	*(to MARY 2)* So where do you come from?
MARY 2	My mother.
JOAN	Art. Leave her alone.
ART	But she's funny.
JOAN	Yeah, but I'm your wife. And I have a bad feeling about this place.
ROBYN	Please... we know what we're doing in here. You have to trust us.

JOAN   Oh is that right?

ART   *(walking with LEO hand in hand)* You gotta
                a pretty big mitt there fella.

LEO   First base gotta have a good trapper right
                foot on the bag... he's outta there!

ART   Loved shortstop myself.

LEO   Si Manuel. Si.

ART   You ever played cricket?

LEO   No, but I swallowed one once.

ART   You're kidding me.

LEO   Maybe.

ART   *(beat)* Oh.

LEO   You want to knock some flies out to me?

ART   *(suspiciously)* What kind of flies?

JOAN   Art, please stop.

ART   Oh come on, Joan... we're talking sports
                over here. I think.

JOAN   We have more pressing issues.

                *JOAN goes to her father who has wandered
                into view holding a piece of a small copper
                pipe.*

JOAN   What's going on, father? You okay?

MICHAEL   Don't bother me. I'm busy.

JOAN   I'm thinking of taking you home.

MICHAEL   What?

JOAN   You deserve better.

MICHAEL   I deserve what I deserve. Don't you get
smart with me. Now get me a Coke, will
you?

JOAN   *(to ART)* You see?

ART   Look, as long as you're going to get a
Coke anyway, could you pick me up some
Raisinettes?

JOAN   No!

> *GABRIELLE enters. MICHAEL joins her
> and they bump into each other. They look
> at each other carefully.*

GABRIELLE   Hello.

MICHAEL   Hello.

> *ART and JOAN watch.*

ART   *(to JOAN)* Come on. It's okay.

JOAN   I hope he's all right in here.

ART   Look at him. He's fine. He's making a
friend. Let's go.

MICHAEL   Well...

GABRIELLE   Well, well...

> *ART, JOAN and the others fade into the
> background.*

GABRIELLE   You bumped into me.

MICHAEL   Who?

GABRIELLE   Me! You bumped into me, mister.

MICHAEL   What do you want me to do about it?

GABRIELLE   Don't yell at me. I'm the bumpee.
Not the bumper.

MICHAEL   I'm not yelling. What's with you people
in here?!
Are you crazy?

GABRIELLE   What about it?

MICHAEL   The whole world is crazy upside down.

GABRIELLE   Well don't blame me. You bumped into
me and that's a fact.

MICHAEL   This is an impossible situation.
Impossible! What is this place?

GABRIELLE   Don't get huffy with me.

MICHAEL   Who are you?

GABRIELLE   Who's asking?

MICHAEL   Listen, I have a right to know.

GABRIELLE   I'm not sure I like your tone.

MICHAEL   Who are you!?

GABRIELLE   Look, I'm warning you—

MICHAEL   WHO ARE YOU?!

GABRIELLE   Now you're yelling again.

MICHAEL   *(yelling)* ARRRRRRGGGGH!

> MICHAEL *picks up a chair and throws it.*
> *A moment.*

GABRIELLE Well, I'm glad I wasn't sitting in that.

MICHAEL Look, we've met before. I know it.

GABRIELLE Yes, it's true.

MICHAEL And so...?

GABRIELLE *(beat, unsure of what to do)* I don't know.

MICHAEL *(pausing, he wants to punch something, then suddenly)* O God! I could be bounded in a nut-shell and count myself a king of infinite space, were it not that I have bad dreams. *(beat)* Oh shit. That's not it.

GABRIELLE *(after a moment)* You have a grand voice, you know that. It's like a thunderclap.

MICHAEL But I don't know... I don't know...

GABRIELLE But what a voice. *(nothing, then finally, to herself)* You're welcome. Thank-you.

  VIRGIL enters.

VIRGIL Hi.

MICHAEL Oh don't "hi" me.

VIRGIL I've just come for my wife.

MICHAEL Nobody here but us.

VIRGIL Right.

MICHAEL So just mind your own business.

VIRGIL All right. Just take it easy, old-timer. Come on, Gabby. Time to go.

MICHAEL Hold on there. What's this all about?

VIRGIL	Just relax, she'll be back...
MICHAEL	Korea. Served with the UN. So watch yourself.
VIRGIL	I will.
MICHAEL	Where are you taking her?
VIRGIL	Home. For a visit.
MICHAEL	You're taking her away, aren't you?
GABRIELLE	I'll be fine. Don't worry.
MICHAEL	You know me, don't you? Please...
GABRIELLE	You have a grand voice. Gives me shivers—
VIRGIL	*(interrupting)* Let's go sweetheart.
GABRIELLE	*(to VIRGIL)* You... you dress like a salesman. An unsuccessful knife man. What's your business here?
VIRGIL	I'm your husband, Gabrielle.
GABRIELLE	Oh my God... how did that happen?
MICHAEL	You bring her back in one piece, mister.
VIRGIL	I'll remember that. See you partner, gotta go, running late.
MICHAEL	I'm an educated man, you understand?
VIRGIL	You betcha.
MICHAEL	See you soon. Watch your purse, love.
GABRIELLE	Yes, yes... you too.

MICHAEL   I'll be right here.

> *VIRGIL leaves with GABRIELLE on his arm. GABRIELLE looks back at MICHAEL ever so briefly.*
>
> *MICHAEL is left alone. He looks around trying to figure out where exactly he is. He doesn't really know.*

MICHAEL   Shit.

> *Suddenly other Alzheimer's patients enter. They confuse MICHAEL. He tries to look cool.*
>
> *MICHAEL finds a pipe in his pocket and takes it out. He puts it in his mouth and tries to look proud and academic. The others look at him.*

MICHAEL   Anybody got a match?

> *They turn away.*

MICHAEL   Anybody?!

> *No response.*

MICHAEL   How about you? You got a light?

> *No response.*

MICHAEL   What's with you people?

> *No answer. Pause.*

MICHAEL   Suit yourselves.

> *Michael pretends to take a match out of his pocket and strikes it.*

MICHAEL   OUCH!!

> *The others smile. MICHAEL has finally got a response out of them.*

MICHAEL　Ha. *(beat)* Idiots.

> *Finally JOAN enters carrying a scarf. She holds it out for him.*

JOAN　Thought you could use this. It's cold out tonight.

MICHAEL　You know, I think we should go to the lake again.

JOAN　Yes, yes... that would be great.

MICHAEL　Sailboats as far as the eye can see. Blue, white and green.

JOAN　We have to get insulation, it's freezing at night.

MICHAEL　Got to cozy up to stay warm. Read some poetry. Drink some tea. Oh yes... good times are hard to find today.

JOAN　We can still have some good times.

MICHAEL　Of course we can. Let's just do it!

> *He hugs her. JOAN seems surprised.*

JOAN　You've never done that before. That was really nice.

MICHAEL　Yes... yes... well, there you have it. Why are you here and not out having fun?

JOAN　Because I'm the only one left.

MICHAEL　Oh. *(beat)* You're going to turn out just like me. I know it.

Music up.

MICHAEL   Now there's a tune! Come on, let's cut a rug.

MICHAEL grabs JOAN.

JOAN   Dad, do you mind?

MICHAEL   Quick... what happens when two accountants marry?

JOAN   What?

MICHAEL   I don't know... there's no punch line.

JOAN   Don't make fun of me, okay?

MICHAEL   Well don't end up like me, okay? I don't want to be an old man in an old folk's home who gets monthly visits from a daughter who's as dry as dust. Old is boring enough.

MICHAEL awkwardly forces her to dance.

JOAN   Look, we're not at home, dad... we're in the clinic. Do you understand?

MICHAEL realizes this and the music fades.

MICHAEL   Oh my god... oh my god... where's my pipe?

JOAN   Here.

JOAN gets his pipe out of his pocket for him.

JOAN   You're going to be okay, father

MICHAEL jams the pipe in his mouth.

MICHAEL   Like hell I am. *(beat)* I once knew a girl with a beautiful smile. She was my girl. Until she was taken away.

JOAN   You talking about me or Rachael?

MICHAEL   The most beautiful girl in the whole wide world.

JOAN   Father, look at me.

MICHAEL   After my own heart.

JOAN   Please father, look at me. It's Joan.

MICHAEL   Nope. Something's wrong, kid.

JOAN   *(beat)* What?

MICHAEL   Gotta go.

MICHAEL shuffles away.

JOAN   I need you dad. Please... don't go.

MICHAEL stops, then shuffles away.

JOAN   Don't do this to me, father! Father?!

MICHAEL stops. He turns to her with his pipe.

MICHAEL   For the last time... do you have a god-damn light?

Lights fade.

Projection: "A Butterfly flaps its wings once and the air all over the earth is changed forever."
          — Old Chinese proverb

ACT ONE
Scene Six

Lights up on VIRGIL at home as he helps
GABRIELLE eat mashed bananas.

GABRIELLE   Ugh!

VIRGIL   They're just mashed bananas.

GABRIELLE   Bugs in there.

VIRGIL   Come on, raisins. That's all.

GABRIELLE   Get that away from me.

VIRGIL   Here we go, one more.

              GABRIELLE swats it away.

              You know, I think you need a bath.

GABRIELLE   No.

VIRGIL   Come on... it's not like we haven't had
              baths together before.

              VIRGIL pulls GABRIELLE toward the
              "bathroom" which is a black and white tile
              effect. GABRIELLE sees this and freaks
              out.

GABRIELLE   No! No! No!

VIRGIL   What?

GABRIELLE   Horrible! Awful!

VIRGIL   Come on, it's just the bathroom.

GABRIELLE   *(terrified)* Ahhhhhh!

> *Suddenly NETTY walks in.*

NETTY   Mom? You okay?

GABRIELLE Terrible!

NETTY   What's going on, dad?

VIRGIL   I was just going to give her a bath. She took one look in there and starting yelling. Come here, Gabby.

GABRIELLE No!

> *GABRIELLE slaps VIRGIL. A stunned moment.*

NETTY   It's okay mom.

GABRIELLE Awful man.

VIRGIL   I told you this would happen.

NETTY   Go for a walk.

VIRGIL   I'll take my time.

> *VIRGIL leaves.*

NETTY   Well that was something, wasn't it?

GABRIELLE Yes. Terrible thing. Bathroom...

NETTY   It must have been quite a mess in there.

GABRIELLE Holes. Holes in the walls.
And water...
Water everywhere...

NETTY   Yeah, I guess it does look like holes in there. But you really shouldn't have whacked dad like that. Look at you, you're a mess.

> *She points her toward a mirror.*
> *GABRIELLE is frightened of who she sees.*

GABRIELLE NO!

NETTY What is it mother?

GABRIELLE Who is that?

NETTY That's you.

GABRIELLE No, no, no.

NETTY It is.

GABRIELLE No... I have a nice smile and good teeth. Who is that?

NETTY You do have a nice smile and good teeth.

GABRIELLE *(seeing NETTY's reflection)* And who's that?

NETTY Me.

GABRIELLE *(confused)* Who?

NETTY Your daughter.

GABRIELLE *(looking closer)* She's prettier than me.

NETTY You are still very pretty to me.

GABRIELLE No I'm not.

NETTY I say you are. And so does your husband.

GABRIELLE I don't trust him.

NETTY I know...

GABRIELLE Whacked him good.

NETTY   Yeah, you sure did.

GABRIELLE   Whacked him once after Montserrat.
               Caught him red handed.
               She was prettier than me. Nicer teeth too.

NETTY   What?

GABRIELLE   A redhead from Morris, Manitoba.

NETTY   Dad? Dad did this?

GABRIELLE   He wouldn't stop, couldn't stop.
               All through the years.

NETTY   I can't believe this...

GABRIELLE   You're father is too horny.

NETTY   Oh my God...

GABRIELLE   Oh yes. Horny as hell.

NETTY   I don't believe this.

GABRIELLE   You'll get used to it.

NETTY   My father slept around...

GABRIELLE   And around and around...

NETTY   This is unbelievable...

GABRIELLE He's the kind of man
I should have stayed away from.
But all the women were crazy about him
back then.
Even my mother.
He sure knew how to fill a room.
"Your husband is quite the catch" they'd
all say.
"You're a lucky girl, a very lucky girl..."
And I believed them.
That was my big mistake.
(beat)
But then I look at you now...
You with that face,
And I get a big smile.

　　Lights fade.

GABBY (Doris Chillcott) and NETTY (Susan Chapple): "How's your head?"

ACT ONE
Scene Seven

Lights up on ROBYN, JOAN and
MICHAEL in ROBYN's office.
MICHAEL is wearing "the scarf" now.
JOAN has a notepad. Nearby ART sits
watching as MARY 2 and LEO, who are
dressed in rich colours, paint.

JOAN   I'm taking him out of this facility.

ROBYN   I would advise you to re-consider.

JOAN   He's been here for several months. He's
                not responding any better, he's not
                improving... all he does is wander around
                and mumble under his breath.

ROBYN   Well, he's quite good at it.

JOAN   Don't be flippant.

ROBYN   Occupational hazard. Sorry.

JOAN   What new treatments are available on the
                market?

ROBYN   We're working on many new treatments.
                We've had some success. But I'm afraid
                that your father will still have difficulty
                relating to you on your terms.

JOAN   Same old same old.

ROBYN   I beg your pardon?

JOAN   Look... what can be done specifically to
                improve his memory?

ROBYN   There is a medication to help memory loss but it's more effective in earlier stages of the disease. At this point, though, he can't always orient himself to time or place... or sometimes, even to you.

JOAN   This is ridiculous. You make it sound like he's fallen into a black hole or something. What is with you people?

ROBYN   Believe it or not, it's an epidemic. Sneaking up behind us and quietly wiping out a generation. The wise ones. The ones with all the insight and experience. The ones with the big hearts, the warm laps and the huge photo albums. Would you like to see the statistics?

JOAN   No thank you.

            Focus on ART and MARY 2.

ART   What are you painting?

MARY 2   You.

ART   Well, I like the hair.

MARY 2   Would you like to paint too?

ART   I'm not sure if I'd be any good.

MARY 2   You have an artist's soul, I'm sure.

ART   Really? You can tell?

MARY 2   Tell what?

ART   I have an artist's soul.

MARY 2   Do you?

ART   Uh... I'm confused here. Do I or don't I?

MARY 2	What are you... taking a poll?
ART	No—
LEO	Well start painting and stop jabbering.
ART	I might wreck this, you know.
MARY 2	Why would you think that?
ART	Well, I was a bit of a failure when it came to the arts. No confidence I guess.
MARY 2	Not you.
ART	I'm afraid so. Probably explains why I married... well, who I married.
MARY 2	Is she an artist?
ART	No. Just confident. Way over-confident.
MARY 2	So... who's stopping you from painting anyway?
ART	I don't know...

LEO approaches.

LEO	What's his problem?
MARY 2	Confidence.
ART	Confidence.
LEO	Look you lose your confidence, you can't play the game. Loosen up, kid.
ART	Alright—
LEO	This game is 90 percent mental. The other half is pure luck.

MARY 2   So just throw your brush on there, young
               man, before the paint dries.

ART   Okay... here goes nothing...

               *ART adds to the painting with a long
               swoosh of colour. He stands back and
               admires it. The swoosh looks like the Nike
               running shoe swoosh.*

               Nike. Not great Nike. But good Nike.

MARY 2   Beginner's luck.

               *Focus on ROBYN and JOAN while
               MARY 2 paints a flower over the Nike
               swoosh.*

ROBYN   Taking him out of the facility at this point
               could be dangerous. You can't watch him
               24 hours a day. I'm sure you know that.

JOAN   Don't lecture me, all right? I've studied
               this problem. I've spent weekends in the
               library. I've gone to all the meetings and
               I've met with experts. I know what's
               going on. *(beat)* Boy... I don't think I like
               you, lady.

MICHAEL   I could use a drink over here.

               ROBYN gives him a drink of water.

MICHAEL   Cheap god-damn Scotch.

ROBYN   Good stuff is hard to get. You tried that
               stuff? From Scotland?

MICHAEL   Yes...yes...
               The Black Watch. Devils in dresses.
               Horrific fighters.
               Hear their pipes for miles.
               Nothing but the good stuff for those boys.

> *MICHAEL tries to drink the water but coughs most of it out.*

JOAN   You okay, dad?

ROBYN   He's fine. Just went down the wrong hole, right?

MICHAEL   *(recovering)* Bad rabbit.

ROBYN   *(to MICHAEL)* You need a slap on the back?

MICHAEL   Depends. Who's doing the slapping?

ROBYN   You want to go back to your room?

JOAN   He's not going to his room. Come on dad, we're going home.

ROBYN   Listen, we really should talk more about this—

JOAN   My mind is made up. He's my dad. I'm his daughter. And you people are well-paid and probably very thorough, but you have too many patients.

ROBYN   What's that supposed to mean?

JOAN   You do this kind of work all the time. You see tragedy around you all the time. You don't know... you can't feel what I feel.

ROBYN   Oh gimme a break. That's not true—

JOAN   *(going to her father)* Let's go home, dad.

ROBYN   He will become extremely agitated.

JOAN   He's always been agitated.

ROBYN   Look, the reason you brought him here
               was because he kept wandering away.
               Your house is unfamiliar to him and he
               can't go home anymore. You sold his
               house. What's the man to do? We've
               worked out a routine here. And this rou-
               tine is very important.

JOAN   Well, he can learn a new routine. I can do
               this. I'm very organized.

ROBYN   This isn't just about you.

JOAN   I'm different, you'll see. Come on, dad.

               JOAN tries to grab MICHAEL's water.

JOAN   Leave it alone, dad.

               MICHAEL doesn't.

JOAN   Give it to me.

               *MICHAEL drinks it defiantly then gives
               her the glass. Then he turns to leave.*

ROBYN   Just a minute, Joan. I need you to finish
               some paperwork.

JOAN   What for?

ROBYN   Well, if you're going to take him home.
               It's okay, don't worry about your father.
               This place is made for wandering about.

               JOAN goes to sign the paperwork.

               *Focus on MICHAEL as he finds
               GABRIELLE nearby.*

MICHAEL   Hello over there.

GABRIELLE   Oh I'm not so far away.

MICHAEL   What are you up to?

GABRIELLE   About five foot something. How about
             yourself?

MICHAEL   Well, I've lost a little off the top.

GABRIELLE   Well that's maybe a good thing.
             Your head is pretty big.

MICHAEL   Yes I've been told that before.
             A swollen head... a terrible thing really.
             Too many books and not enough time for
             just visiting.

             I like your dress, madam.
             It reminds me of either a Swiss meadow
             or a fondue, but I don't quite know why.
             What colour is that?

GABRIELLE   I don't know.
             But it makes me feel good.

MICHAEL   Yes, yes... I can see that.

GABRIELLE   Would you like to walk with me?

MICHAEL   Where are we going?

GABRIELLE   Just over there.

MICHAEL   Fine with me.
             Do you have any children?

GABRIELLE   Not on me.

MICHAEL   My daughter is here. She wants to take
             me away.
             I really don't know what to do.

GABRIELLE   Have you tried spanking her?

MICHAEL   I'm afraid she'd break my knees.

GABRIELLE   Is she a big girl?

MICHAEL   No, she's an accountant.

GABRIELLE   That sounds like a bad joke. Should I laugh?

MICHAEL   I'm afraid not. You can't make jokes about accountants, Lord knows I've tried.

    JOAN catches up to them.

JOAN   There you are. Come on, we're leaving.

GABRIELLE   But we were having such a nice time—

JOAN   I'm sorry.

MICHAEL   I wouldn't mind staying.

GABRIELLE   There's lots of room.

JOAN   We have to go. Good bye.

MICHAEL   Take care, love.

GABRIELLE   Good bye. I'll miss you.

    GABRIELLE shuffles off. JOAN gives MICHAEL a look.

JOAN   What is with you?

MICHAEL   I don't know.
Seems like I've been saying good-bye a lot.
And they all have sexy dresses.

JOAN   You're getting a little too old for that kind of stuff, father.

MICHAEL   Nonsense.

> *JOAN spots ART still painting. MARY 2 and LEO watch him.*

JOAN   What in the world is that?

ART   A frog in a blender. *(JOAN gives him a look)* I don't know.

LEO   *(to JOAN)* Hey toots, you wanna put on a party-dress and catch a double-header?! Come on.

JOAN   *(to LEO)* Not right now. *(to ART)* Come on, Art. We're going home.

MICHAEL   Why are we going?

JOAN   You'll be much better off. Trust me.

MICHAEL   But I don't want to go anywhere.

JOAN   It'll be good for us. We're family.

> *JOAN tugs on his arm but MICHAEL doesn't move.*

JOAN   Come on, what's wrong now?

MICHAEL   I don't know.

JOAN   Art, give us a hand into the car.

ART   *(straightening out)* I'm off then.

> *ART leaves with JOAN and MICHAEL. A moment.*

MARY 2   I thought he was a little off too.

> *ROBYN enters.*

ROBYN   Lunch-time everybody. Come on.

LEO   I hope we're having chicken again. I love
               chicken!

               *LEO and ROBYN exit. MARY 2 stands
               there and looks at the painting.
               GABRIELLE wanders over and looks at it
               too.*

MARY 2   It's no Picasso. But it'll do.

GABRIELLE   I don't know why, but suddenly I feel very
               alone.

MARY 2   Oh we all got our stories, don't we?

GABRIELLE   I think I'm in love. It hurts.

MARY 2   Sometimes I don't like to think about
               being in love.

GABRIELLE   Tell me about it, please. It's okay. Life
               goes on.

MARY 2   You sure you have room for another sad
               story?

GABRIELLE   One more.

MARY 2   Well, let's see. My sad story...
               It was a long time ago.
               He was the kind of man you'd love to find
               Asleep on your couch. A slow talker.
               Eyes like a tired wolf.

               *Music comes up and MARY 2 takes
               GABRIELLE's hand.*

GABRIELLE   Where are we going?

MARY 2   Into the dark.

GABRIELLE   Then what happens?

MARY 2   We don't look back.

They slowly walk off into the dark.

Lights fade.

ACT TWO
Scene One

Projection:
"Between the idea and the reality
Between the motion and the act
falls the shadow."
                              — *T. S. Eliot*

Time has passed. Lights up as all enter
wearing their overcoats.

LEO, MARY and MARY 2 and the others
stand on the "bows" of the sailboats. They
sing "Great is thy Faithfulness" (or any
similar hymn).

Great is Thy faithfulness
O God my Father
There is no shadow of turning with Thee
Thou changest not, Thy compassions, they
fail not
As Thou hast been
Thou forever wilt be.

Summer and Winter and spring time and
harvest
Sun moon and stars in their courses above
Join with all nature in manifold witness
To thy great faithfulness, mercy and love.

The lyrics begin to falter...

Pardon my sin...
And a peace that...
Hmmmm, hmmmm, hmmmm...
Strength for today
And bright hope for tomorrow
Da, da, da, da, da-da...
Da, da, da, dee...

They wander, humming a little, until that fades too. They randomly confront each other as if looking for something.

They slowly all exit.

NETTY and VIRGIL enter carrying enormous golf bags on their backs, looking like the weight of the world is upon them. They are at the golf course.

VIRGIL   Did you find it yet?

NETTY   No.

VIRGIL   Try to your left.

VIRGIL   I told you to keep your head down.

NETTY   You haven't answered my question. Did you do it?

VIRGIL   There's a Japanese foursome behind us, Annette. And there's a film crew following them around. Let's keep it moving, alright?

NETTY   Mom said it happened. Is that true?

VIRGIL   Expo, remember? We drove half-way across the country in a white Galaxy 500 and your mother snored the whole way. Now she denies everything. Can't remember this. Can't remember that. In fact, she doesn't think we ever left. Consider your source, Netty.

NETTY   Did it happen, dad? Please tell me.

VIRGIL   God, this grass is long. Won't find anything in here.

NETTY   I really need to know, dad! I have been a good daughter...

VIRGIL   *(overlapping)* I know—

NETTY   ...made sure my priorities were right. Both parents loved and obeyed. Respected and honoured. In fact, married once to the wrong man for the love of my family. Graduated from the wrong program at the wrong university for what was expected. Lived at home as long as I could take it. Nights listening to you two scream at each other from under the floor or through the pipes or in the car on the driveway just because I brought home the wrong person or did the wrong thing or forgot what was really important. Sucking blame into my lungs like I was a marathon runner, over and over. Bawling my eyes out all night, then waking up and finding mom crying in the garden and your razor gone. Weeks of nothing, not even a damn phone call and she still defended you, still wrapped herself in your stupid grey sweater like she was frozen from the inside out. Tell me it's not true. Tell me you were in Alberta building Greystone or Green Fucking Acres. Tell me about honour and commitment and doing the right thing. Tell me about how you screwed up and what happened to my life when I was too young to know better. And don't you dare run away from me.

VIRGIL   *(after a moment)* All right. It's true. All of it.

                 NETTY takes off her golf bag and jams it into VIRGIL's arms.

NETTY   I thought so.

          She exits. A moment.

VIRGIL   Annette? Wait for me. Come on... I can't carry all this.

          No answer. VIRGIL leaves too, struggling with his load.

          Lights fade.

ACT TWO
Scene Two

Lights illuminate GABRIELLE at the facility. She thinks she is sitting under a tree. MARY joins her, carrying a piece of birthday cake on a napkin.

MARY   Happy anniversary, sweetheart.

GABRIELLE   Is it?

MARY   Sure.
Married, what? Forty years?

GABRIELLE   What?

MARY   'Course, who can keep count?

GABRIELLE   *(a little confused)* Yes... I suppose...

MARY   That's my ball and chain
I always say.

GABRIELLE   It sure is. *(beat)* Did you have a good life?

MARY   I think so.

GABRIELLE   At home?

MARY   Home?
But once I was a teacher.

GABRIELLE   Me too.

MARY   All those lesson plans.

GABRIELLE   Oh sure. Enough to fill a closet.

MARY   I had a student named Felix
Who helped invent some gizmo
For the computer.
He killed himself, you know.
No need for that.
You love them all the same.

I had six thousand and fifty students.
Or around that number.
And only six came back.

GABRIELLE   I taught my daughter.

MARY   How wonderful.

GABRIELLE   She's a big girl now.
Very educated.
Used to steal my make-up.
Lipstick I think.

MARY   At college the kids got bigger and bigger
over time.

GABRIELLE   I think they drink too much milk.

MARY   I taught drama.
One day I went to school
And couldn't figure out how to get home.
Pretty soon I got lost in *Macbeth*.
Then *A Midsummer Night's Dream*.
Then *Hamlet*. Then the other stuff...

GABRIELLE   Oh yes... Shakespeare.
I think he was a homosexual.

MARY   Well, each to their own I always say. *(beat)*
I wonder how *his* kids turned out.

GABRIELLE   It's hard to be both a parent and a teacher.

MARY   I know what you're saying. I know...

                I can't teach like I want to.
                I don't go to meetings anymore.
                I can't quote anything... or anyone.
                But I can still bake a cake like nobody's
                business.

GABRIELLE   *(beat)* Listen you...

MARY   Mary.

GABRIELLE   Mary.

MARY   Mary.

GABRIELLE   Mary. I want to scream all night.
                I want to scream and scream and scream.
                Why?

                        MARY holds out the cake.

MARY   Take.
                Eat.

                        GABRIELLE finally takes a bite.

GABRIELLE   *(eating)* Thanks... what's your name...?

MARY   Don't. Please.
                I'll just cry.
                And I've run out.

                        MARY leaves.

                        Lights fade.

MARY (Sheila Paterson) and GABRIELLE (Doris Chilcott): "I had six thousand and fifty students."

ACT TWO
Scene Three

*Lights up on ART, JOAN and MICHAEL
at home. JOAN is putting Post-It notes on
things. As soon as JOAN puts them up,
MICHAEL, following behind, picks them
up and sticks them to his forehead.*

*ART walks around with an electric guitar
strapped to him, trying to learn chords.
He's new at this, but he's trying.*

ART   Overboard, Joan. Totally overboard.

JOAN   Well, at least I'm doing something.

ART   You heard of rock and roll, baby?

JOAN   You're almost 60 Art, put down the guitar
before some kids see you.

ART   Wouldn't that be something.

JOAN   Where did you get these crazy notions?

ART   Hey I figure you're never too late. Keeps
the brain juices circulating.

JOAN   Your brain juices don't need circulating.
Help me put these stickies up.

He takes one and sticks it to his guitar.

*JOAN notices MICHAEL has stickies
stuck to his head.*

Come on, dad... concentrate.

ART plays a chord on his guitar.

ART	Wow.
JOAN	That's horrible. Why can't you blow a horn or something?
ART	I have bad lips. They chap.
JOAN	Now dad, pay attention here. What is this?

> *JOAN points to a blank screen (sail).*

MICHAEL	Well...
JOAN	This is the phone.
MICHAEL	Oh yeah...
JOAN	And what's that over there?

> *Pointing to another blank screen.*

MICHAEL	Well...
JOAN	Toaster. And that? *(no answer)* Microwave.
MICHAEL	Micro-zap.
JOAN	Wave.

> *MICHAEL waves and walks away.*

JOAN	No, no... I'm not done. What's this? *(pointing to another screen)*
ART	*(singing)* "Love... love... love... love is all you need... yeah..."
JOAN	DO YOU MIND?
ART	What?

JOAN   .   Try to tune in for a minute, Ringo.

ART   Well you're no fun.

JOAN   Then why'd you marry me?

A moment. ART thinks.

ART   Uh... give me a second here...

MICHAEL walks over and sticks a stickie on ART's forehead.

ART notices MICHAEL has one stuck to his forehead too.

ART   Well what do you know. Nice to meet you... uh... toaster.

JOAN   Oh just get out of here. And put on a headset. I don't want to hear that noise.

JOAN takes the sticky off ART's forehead.

ART   Noise?! It's rock, baby. Get with the tour.

JOAN   I'll get with the tour when they bring my bus around, but until then I'll act my age.

ART   Suit yourself... I'm gonna rock.

ART puts on a headset. JOAN takes the sticky off MICHAEL's forehead.

JOAN   This doesn't belong here.

MICHAEL suddenly doesn't recognize ART with his headset on.

JOAN looks around the place trying to figure out where to put the sticky. ART pinches her playfully, MICHAEL sees this. It's upsetting to him.

JOAN   Ouch!

MICHAEL   *(to ART)* Hey!

JOAN   What now?

MICHAEL   Hey you!

         ART turns around.

ART   What's up, poppa bear?

MICHAEL   You stay away from my daughter!

ART   What?

MICHAEL   Stay away!

ART   We're married, come on.

MICHAEL   GET AWAY FROM HER! MOVE IT!

ART   *(to JOAN)* I think I'll be sleeping on the couch tonight.

JOAN   Dad? Are you okay?

         MICHAEL raises his hand to slap her.

MICHAEL   You should know better... you... you...!
I'm an educated man.
I know what's going on.
You can't treat me this way.
I won't have it.
Where is she? Where?!

JOAN   Who? What are you talking about, dad?
Dad? Dad look at me when I'm talking to you.

MICHAEL   *(confused)* Uhh... she... her... uhh...

JOAN   I'm your daughter, right? A nice girl, remember? Studied hard and... Art... you know Art? My husband? The boring chartered accountant I ended up with? We're at home and that's all there is.

MICHAEL   I'm hungry. I'm always hungry. When are we going to eat?

JOAN   Soon.

MICHAEL   Make my steak rare. Alright?

JOAN   Right dad.

Lights fade on them.

ACT TWO
Scene Four

Lights up on NETTY, VIRGIL and GABRIELLE at the facility.

VIRGIL Look, this is a bad idea.

NETTY I don't care. If you're seeing someone else... she might as well know.

VIRGIL Why now of all times? It's wrong.

NETTY Don't you dare tell me what's right and wrong.

VIRGIL It's what your mother would want. If she was here.

NETTY She is here.

VIRGIL Right. *(beat)* I'm asking you, please... let's not pursue this—

GABRIELLE *(louder and overlapping)* Ohhhh...

VIRGIL Look, she's really upset.

NETTY I wonder why.

VIRGIL You're doing this to her.

NETTY ME!?

GABRIELLE bangs her shoes together.

NETTY Mother, are you okay? What are you doing?

GABRIELLE If you tap your shoes together, you can go home.

VIRGIL   *(beat)* Maybe I'll take her outside for a walk.

NETTY   Go then!

VIRGIL   I will.

> *VIRGIL takes GABRIELLE and they move away.*
>
> *NETTY watches them. Lighting changes as something about the way VIRGIL holds GABBY's arm reminds NETTY of how things used to be. It's a flashback.*
>
> *VIRGIL is trying to show GABRIELLE how to swing a golf club.*

VIRGIL   Keep your head down and follow through, Gabby.

> *He holds the club and her from behind. GABRIELLE jumps a bit.*

GABRIELLE   Keep poking me like that and I'll have to get a new coach.

VIRGIL   Sorry. Got a little flutter in my putter.

GABRIELLE   Hey, smell my roses.

VIRGIL   Hmmm. You've done a great job out here.

GABRIELLE   I love my house. I never want to leave this place.

VIRGIL   What are those flowers around the steps?

GABRIELLE   Hydrangea. They change colour. But it depends on what's in the soil.

VIRGIL   How'd you get so smart?

GABRIELLE   I'm a woman. It comes naturally.

> *Lighting changes. NETTY's happy memory disintegrates as she watches GABRIELLE and VIRGIL shuffle away in real time.*

GABRIELLE   Where am I?

VIRGIL   Home.

GABRIELLE   *(exiting)* Where am I?

VIRGIL   *(exiting)* Home, love.

> *They exit.*

> *Lights fade.*

ACT TWO
Scene Five

Lights up on JOAN and MICHAEL at home. She's trying to give him a drink of water. He drinks some and then she pulls away the glass.

JOAN   Ask me for it and I'll give you the water.

MICHAEL reaches for the water.

JOAN   Ask me!

MICHAEL reaches again, but she pulls it away again.

JOAN   Come on! If I was your Rachael you'd ask for it, wouldn't you?! Ask me!

MICHAEL grabs her arm and JOAN pulls it away. MICHAEL lets go and the water goes flying over JOAN. ART enters.

JOAN   He's not co-operating.

ART   He's not supposed to.

JOAN   He's getting worse. He hardly talks. And he pissed himself this morning.

ART   Well... it's happening then.

JOAN   We can manage it.

ART   Are you kidding? Come on, we're out of our league here. Are you eating? Are you sleeping? *(no answer)* I didn't think so.

JOAN   I'm not a quitter!

ART   Stop it. Come on! He's not going to
               change. He's drifting, Joan. And the
               ocean is getting bigger by the minute.
               Look at his face. Is he looking back at
               you? Is he? You can't run after him, teach
               him or train him like he's some kind of
               god-damn circus animal. It's wrong.
               Anyway, what about *my* needs? What
               about us? Don't you think we're forget-
               ting about that a little?

JOAN   He will get better, Art. I can do it.

ART   Get over it Joan. Take a break and live
               your life. Your father is not going to come
               back. And neither is your lost childhood.
               You go find it.

JOAN   I love my father.

ART   Do you? Give him the god-damned water,
               Joan.

               *JOAN gives MICHAEL the water and he
               tries to drink it. He sputters and spills.*

JOAN   Oh dad. I'm afraid... what am I going to
               do? What am I going to do?

ART   It's time, Joan... I'll call the facility and
               we'll...

               *JOAN suddenly takes the glass from
               MICHAEL and exits.*

ART   ...set the sails. *(beat)* Some life this is turn-
               ing out to be. I don't know who's cra-
               zier... you, me, or my wife?

               You're not going to answer, are you?
               (beat) Maybe that's a good thing.

ART   (continuing) Mad as hatters. All because
             of this... thing. I can't even say it some
             days. I'm tired of thinking about it and
             being the strong one and... playing the
             game. Well, I guess you're not the only
             one who has it. We all have it. And
             there's no getting away from it, is there?

             (beat) Got any suggestions, captain?

MICHAEL   Byzantium.

ART   Is that the place for us?

MICHAEL   "That is no country for old men. The
             young
             In one another's arms, birds in the trees
             —Those dying generations—at their song,
             The salmon-falls, the mackerel-crowded
             seas,
             Fish, flesh, or fowl, commend all summer
             long
             Whatever is begotten, born, and dies."
             (beat) I think that was a poem.

ART   Hey I thought you were talking about the
             Rolling Stones...

MICHAEL   The who?

ART   No the Stones...

MICHAEL   Yes... of course...

ART   The Who are mostly deaf.

MICHAEL   Whaddya say?

ART   Deaf!

MICHAEL   Who's deaf?

ART   That's right. Wait a minute... I think we're
             doing a routine, mister.

MICHAEL   Who is?

ART   Very funny... let's go. We need a couple of
             stiff drinks. I'll make you a Caesar. How
             'bout that?

             They start exiting.

MICHAEL   *(beat)* Caesar who?

             ART laughs.

             Lights fade.

ACT TWO
Scene Six

Music swells.

> *Lights up on ROBYN in the facility. She's dancing with MARY 2, who is even more colourfully dressed. LEO enters with GABRIELLE.*

ROBYN Round and round she goes... very good, everybody... you people look wonderful today.

LEO We always look wonderful today.

GABRIELLE Do you know where that nice man is?

ROBYN Are you looking for Michael, Gabrielle?

GABRIELLE Is that his name?

ROBYN Yes.

GABRIELLE An angel, right?

ROBYN Sure. Why not?

GABRIELLE I once read a book on angels.
I forget how it ended...
But they all had such nice tans,
"Bronze skin and flaxen hair."
Handsome devils.

LEO I hate the Angels.
A lousy team if you ask me.
No pitching.
No speed.
And crappy uniforms.

> *Suddenly MARY enters. ROBYN sees her.*

ROBYN   Look! We have a visitor.
                 She's beautiful.

MARY takes off her overcoat revealing a long white sleeping garment.

Other Alzheimer's patients drift in.

The music stops. So does the dancing.

MARY   I'm frightened.

ROBYN   It's okay, Mary.

MARY   How do I look?

ROBYN   Absolutely beautiful.

MARY   Thank-you. *(beat)* What will happen to me?

ROBYN   I don't know. None of us do.

MARY   But it's my time, isn't it?

ROBYN   Yes. I suppose.

MARY   It just snuck up on me, didn't it?

ROBYN nods and takes the overcoat from MARY.

ROBYN   Are you ready?

MARY   Yes. But there should be music playing.
                 Something from Chopin and Mozart or...
                 or...
                 Well, it would be grand.
                 Any music... please...

ROBYN   Okay Mary.

> *ROBYN waves her hand and almost magically classical music swells.*

MARY Oh no.... something else.

> *ROBYN waves her hand and the music changes, it's much grander classical music.*

MARY Much better. Perfect for a grand exit. Wouldn't you say?

> *MARY waltzes away dancing with each before fading into the dark.*
>
> *MICHAEL shuffles out as if looking for someone or something.*
>
> *He spots GABRIELLE and she runs to him. They go to sit.*

MICHAEL I like your dress.
Taffeta?

GABRIELLE No. Gabardine.

MICHAEL Gabardine for Gabby.

GABRIELLE You remembered my name.

MICHAEL Educated man.

GABRIELLE Yes.

MICHAEL I never forget a pretty face.

GABRIELLE Thank-you.

> *A moment. MICHAEL pulls out his pipe.*

GABRIELLE Oh I love a man with a pipe.

MICHAEL Thank you.

GABRIELLE George Bernard Shaw smoked a pipe and lived to his nineties.

MICHAEL Yes and married very late.

GABRIELLE Better late than never.

MICHAEL Right, right.
Just like us.

GABRIELLE Yes, yes...

   A moment.

MICHAEL Oh but your life will be filled with books.
Meetings. Lunch at the faculty club.
(beat) My assistant throws pots in her spare time.

GABRIELLE Are you a hard man to work for?

MICHAEL No. I don't think so. *(beat)*
Ever been to London?

GABRIELLE Of course.
Still have a sister there.
Tea and crumpets. Nice gardens.
Wonderful city.
Filthy of course, the food... worse.
Water terrible.
And all that traffic... horrible, really.
The tubes are nice though.
And the museums.

MICHAEL The British Museum...
Yes. Old books under glass. Yellow pages.
Sonnets, romance, and so on...

GABRIELLE I know you, don't I?

MICHAEL Yes. For a long time, I'm sure.

GABRIELLE   And Michael is in the Good Book, right?

MICHAEL   Yes.

GABRIELLE   Good.

MICHAEL   How do you think we'll end up?

GABRIELLE   Hold my hand. Don't let go. Never let go.

MICHAEL   All right. Why.

GABRIELLE   I know what happens in here.

MICHAEL   Yes. People always coming and going.

GABRIELLE   Yes. Coming and going. *(beat)* Would you like some tea?

MICHAEL   Fine. Where?

GABRIELLE   Follow me.

MICHAEL   Where are we going? Where?!

GABRIELLE   Just there...

MICHAEL   Oh. I might need your arm.

> *GABRIELLE and MICHAEL, arm in arm, shuffle away but they move slower until they stop and sway a bit, almost as if stuck.*

> *LIGHTS UP on NETTY who's watching this with VIRGIL.*

VIRGIL   What stage are we in now? How long has it been? *(no response)* Well at least she's made a friend, I kind of like the old guy.

NETTY   He's about your age, you know.

VIRGIL	At least I'm acting my age.
NETTY	*(coldly)* Since when?

VIRGIL walks over to GABRIELLE.

VIRGIL	Hi honey, how's it going?
NETTY	Get away from me. I have no money.
VIRGIL	It's me, Virgil — your one and only.
MICHAEL	Back off, mister! Or I'll give you one of these!
VIRGIL	*(retreating)* Right... okay... okay... take it easy...

GABRIELLE beams at MICHAEL who still has a fist raised.

GABRIELLE	Oh... that was terrific.
MICHAEL	Thank-you.
GABRIELLE	I'm so lucky. *(to VIRGIL)* You dirty rotter! Good riddance.

MICHAEL and GABRIELLE exit.

VIRGIL	*(beat, then to NETTY)* Well, I guess it's obvious. I've lost out to another man.
NETTY	Lucky for you.
VIRGIL	Look, I thought I should tell you... me and my friend, we have this trip planned.
NETTY	Who?
VIRGIL	Sheila... my girlfriend... she's a realtor.
NETTY	*(sarcastically)* Wonderful.

VIRGIL   And she paints. Flowers mainly but she's thinking about people too. *(beat)* We need a break, that's all. Hawaii. Big empty beaches, blue skies, not a worry in the world. That's what Sheila wanted... so off we go...

NETTY   Fine. I'll be here.

VIRGIL   Listen, I'm no good at loving your mom in bits and pieces. I'm sorry. *(beat)* This is the number where Sheila and me are staying. They say it's beside a black beach and when there's a full moon you can see a million eyes looking back at you. I don't know why I picked it. It didn't look all that romantic in the book and I can't even imagine walking on it. But, what the hell, I think I'll give it a shot.

            Beat.

            You okay about this?

NETTY   Write me a post card.

VIRGIL   *(giving up)* I should go. We'll get together when I get back, what do you say? Dinner? My treat? *(no answer)* Right. If she asks... well, I'm sure you know what to do.

            VIRGIL exits as lights fade.

ACT TWO
Scene Seven

*Lights up on MICHAEL and GABRIELLE
sitting at the facility.*

MICHAEL   We might as well face the facts.

A moment. GABRIELLE gets up.

GABRIELLE   Yes.
How long?

MICHAEL   Just pray... a moment of clarity.

GABRIELLE   You sound clear to me.

MICHAEL   Not clear on anything.
Except you.

GABRIELLE   And we just met.

MICHAEL   Yes, that's the story all right.
(beat) Any other time...
Well, who knows.

GABRIELLE   I know.

MICHAEL   You do?

GABRIELLE   Yes. I can feel it.

MICHAEL   Me too.

Music up.

*LEO and MARY 2 enter dancing. They go
to GABRIELLE and MICHAEL.*

LEO   What are you two doing sitting here like
two frogs on a log?

MICHAEL   Toads sit on logs, frogs sit in water.

LEO   You calling me crazy?!

MICHAEL   Well if the shoe fits.

LEO   *(exploding)* You shut your gob, or I'll take your head like this and shove it up your ass!

MARY 2   *(trying to defuse him)* Please, can we just dance?

LEO   *(to MARY 2)* What do you want?

MARY 2   A dance with a very handsome man.

LEO   *(calming)* Well... well why didn't you say so.

> *LEO takes her and dances away. A moment as MICHAEL and GABRIELLE watch other Alzheimer's patients enter dancing.*

GABRIELLE   That's our song.

MICHAEL   Never heard it before in my life.

GABRIELLE   Perfect... perfect...

> *MICHAEL smiles at her.*

MICHAEL   Would you?

> *GABRIELLE smiles back.*

GABRIELLE   Yes...

> *They shuffle/dance together as the music builds.*

*Other characters, including the chorus,
join them; all suffer from Alzheimer's.
They are wearing masks and more elabo-
rately coloured clothing as if they are at a
surreal masquerade dance.*

*The dancers switch partners and
MICHAEL and GABRIELLE are separat-
ed. They don't recognize anyone they are
dancing with and they start to lose track of
each other especially as the dancers switch
partners back and forth.*

*The music becomes somewhat distorted and
dreamy and the dance becomes haunting
and less unified. It's not so much of a
dance as it is a search or a struggle.*

*MICHAEL searches in vain for
GABRIELLE studying his dance partners
until they suddenly switch around. This
confuses and frustrates him even more.
Without realizing it, though, he is again
dancing with GABRIELLE.*

*The other characters eventually start drop-
ping off, leaving the scene, hunched over
and shuffling.*

*MICHAEL and GABRIELLE are left alone
again, just as they started.*

The music fades.

MICHAEL and GABRIELLE tire.

They stop.

MICHAEL   You all right?

GABRIELLE   Where...? What happened?

MICHAEL   I don't know. *(beat)* Come.

MICHAEL offers his hand in dance.

GABRIELLE   Is there music?

MICHAEL   Yes.

> *In the silence, they try to dance again. But they end up merely shuffling around slowly, bent over and aged beyond their years. But they hold onto each other like they are the last two humans on earth.*
>
> *Lights fade.*

ACT TWO
Scene Eight

Lights up on ROBYN and JOAN at the facility. MICHAEL is nearby.

JOAN
(to MICHAEL) How are you feeling today, dad? *(no response)* They treating you alright? *(he pushes her away and she turns to ROBYN)* Sometimes I think maybe he should just go to sleep and not wake up.

ROBYN
If it happens, do you want us to bring him back?

JOAN
To what?

ROBYN hands over a form. JOAN looks it over.

JOAN
A release. How appropriate.

ROBYN
I like to think of it as a promise.

JOAN
He thinks he's so smart, so tough. I remember when I was 11, he took me to some convention in his old Cadillac. It was a long drive. Nothing but fences and telephone wires. I had a fever. Mumps, I think. I must have fallen asleep. Then I heard WHACK! I woke up. He was slapping himself to stay awake. WHACK! He started his swing from the floor, hard enough you'd think to kill somebody.

MICHAEL raises his hand as if to slap himself. His hand drops.

JOAN   *(continuing)* Anyway, I started crying. He
        pulled over, middle of nowhere, not a
        sound except the rain tapping the roof and
        you know what he said, "Sorry kid, gotta
        get you home fast, you're sick." And I
        saw one side of his face was very red, like
        someone held an iron to it. I thought that
        it was all my fault. I don't know why but
        I did. *(beat)* He's not going to get better,
        is he?

        Well... when will it all happen?

ROBYN   I don't know.

JOAN   I just don't want any pain. *(signing the
        release)*

ROBYN   Do you want to be there when it happens?

JOAN   You're very pushy for a nurse, is that nor-
        mal?

ROBYN   Well, some people find it... a good thing to
        be there. It helps with the transition.

JOAN   Transition? How contemporary. I still
        don't like you. Sorry. You're a little too
        perfect for me. You should be a TV host
        or something.

ROBYN   Look, let me tell you something, the first
        time I experienced someone's death I was
        really scared. When I walked into her
        room, the first thing I noticed was the air.
        Like I had walked into a snowy forest.
        When I moved, it seemed like I was push-
        ing all the molecules around me. I
        stopped to allow myself to breathe. Her
        face was almost like a plaster model of a
        face. One eye half open. A strand of hair
        hung down across her forehead.

ROBYN   (*continuing*) Her mouth was open and
               every time she breathed, that strand of
               hair moved a little. I reached over to
               brush it away. At that very moment, the
               second I touched her head, she sighed. It
               was so soft and so pure I was sure it had
               come from the radio. I pulled my hand
               away, and that was it. She stopped
               breathing. Just like that. And everything
               stopped. No sound outside. No cars, no
               passing buses. One moment as she passed
               on... being nothing more than that. A
               moment. As clear as a bell. And as long
               as her sigh.

JOAN   (*beat*) I suppose you get used to it — you
               people in here. You have so many
               patients—

ROBYN   Actually... that was my mother. I was 14.

JOAN   That isn't fair. I didn't know.

ROBYN   And you don't get used to it and it doesn't
               get easier. Not really.

JOAN   I have to go.

               JOAN exits as the lights fade.

ACT TWO
Scene Nine

*We hear birds chirping. Lights up on
NETTY and GABRIELLE shuffling
around and around in a garden at the facility. GABRIELLE hangs on to NETTY for
dear life.*

NETTY   Either you're shrinking or I'm growing.

GABRIELLE   Yup.

NETTY   How's your head?

GABRIELLE   Fine, fine, fine...

NETTY   The nurse told me you took quite a fall
               yesterday.

GABRIELLE   No I didn't. Look!

NETTY   Yes. Look at those roses. They're very
               pretty.

GABRIELLE   A rose is a rose is a rose...

NETTY   You're a rose.

GABRIELLE   Oh no... not me.

NETTY   Sure you are.

               LEO enters shuffling toward them.

LEO   Excuse me. Are you my fiancee?

NETTY   No.

LEO   Do you know my fiancee?

NETTY   I don't think so.

LEO   So you haven't seen her?

NETTY   No, I'm sorry.

LEO   I was supposed to come for her.

NETTY   Oh—

LEO   If you see her... well, I'll be just over there.

NETTY   Right.

LEO   Thank you for all your help.
It's nice to run into you like this.
Good-bye.

NETTY   Good-bye.

> *LEO shuffles away and then exits. A
> moment.*

NETTY   Well, he was very polite, wasn't he?

GABRIELLE   Who are you?

NETTY   Remember your daughter? The one that always got in trouble?

GABRIELLE   Oh yeah. Little brat.

NETTY   Wasn't she something?

GABRIELLE   She sure was.

NETTY   A good girl though, right?

GABRIELLE   A real sweetheart. Smart as a whip.

NETTY   Could fool everybody I guess.

GABRIELLE   Everybody but her mom.
             Used to take my lipstick to school in her
             lunch-kit. But I just went along.

NETTY   Yeah that's what I thought.
             (beat) I should talk to you about dad... *(no*
             reaction) Virgil? Your husband?

GABRIELLE   Who?!

NETTY   Not much of a husband I'm afraid. He
             even admits it, that's the sad part.

GABRIELLE   Well, your father knows best.

NETTY   Yeah, for once. Listen ma... he wants me
             to meet the redhead. His girlfriend. I
             don't know what to do.

GABRIELLE   Always speak clearly.

NETTY   Yes I know.

GABRIELLE   Don't mumble.

NETTY   It's going to be weird... but I guess it's par
             for the course.

GABRIELLE   Look him straight in the eye.

NETTY   I will.

GABRIELLE   And tell him to be happy.
             It's what your father deserves.

NETTY   Okay.

GABRIELLE   And you make sure to visit your mother
             regularly.

NETTY   Right.

GABRIELLE   And bring her flowers from the garden.
            And chocolate. Lots and lots of chocolate.

NETTY   I'll make sure to do that.

GABRIELLE   And songs.

NETTY   Oh?

GABRIELLE   "When Irish eyes are smiling..."

NETTY   Yeah... well we're Estonian...

GABRIELLE   Yes... terrible thing...

NETTY   It's okay we turned out alright.

GABRIELLE   Good.

NETTY   You know, I hope I'm like you when I get
            your age.

GABRIELLE   Oh?

NETTY   Well, not exactly like you, but close
            enough.

GABRIELLE   Close enough.

            NETTY hugs GABRIELLE.

NETTY   You're shrinking on me, ma.

            *NETTY squeezes her, GABRIELLE groans
            a bit, then coughs.*

NETTY   Sorry.

GABRIELLE   Too close...

NETTY   Got carried away, sorry—

GABRIELLE *(interrupting)* Say hi to your mother when
you see her.

> *GABRIELLE shuffles away, sits and
> slumps. NETTY stands there for a
> moment. Finally NETTY goes to
> GABRIELLE. She leans over and kisses
> her mother.*

NETTY My mother says "hi."

GABRIELLE Oh? Hi.

NETTY Hi.

> *NETTY turns and walks away, stopping
> momentarily to look back at her mother.
> Then she leaves with the smallest of waves.*
>
> *LEO shuffles toward her wearing a big
> coat. He turns on the radio. We hear old
> time music.*
>
> *LEO takes off his big coat. Underneath, an
> old baseball uniform.*
>
> *He pulls out his baseball mitt, he's punch-
> ing a ball into the glove over and over.*
>
> *He strides over to GABRIELLE and tosses
> her the ball but it's attached to his wrist
> with a string and it just hits the floor.*

LEO You think I'm crazy? Do you? Look, I
understand if you don't want to go to
Syracuse. They've called me up. Finally
after all these years. Yeah. I almost gave
up. No kidding. Then out of the blue
Billy Watson, the general manager himself
phones me, tells me I'm his man in the
infield. Me!

LEO   *(beat, then continuing)* I know we've
              planned for a September wedding but it's
              the middle of the season for them and you
              have to understand I've been dreaming of
              this my whole life. It's not that I don't
              love you. Because I do. I love you more
              than anything. But if you don't come with
              me, I just want you to know I will come
              back for Christmas. I will take you in my
              arms and hold you like there's no tomor-
              row. All I ask is that you will be here, just
              like you are now, the same, everything the
              same, so we can fall in love again and
              make it last. I don't know if I could live
              with the fact that I chose baseball over
              you. That would be crazy all right.
              Absolutely crazy.

              (beat) Sweetheart. Listen to me. Listen.
              We will get married, we will live a long
              happy life and the stories we will tell...
              and the stories we will tell...

              *LEO has circled GABRIELLE and has now
              come face to face with the ball in front of
              him. He picks it up and looks once at
              GABRIELLE and then at the ball in the
              glove. He walks away into the dark.*

              *A moment. GABRIELLE looks around and
              spots MICHAEL lying in bed or slumping
              in a chair. She shuffles over to him.*

GABRIELLE   Is it your birthday?

MICHAEL   Whuu-whuu...
              Eight... got a train...
              Whuu-whuu... little light.

GABRIELLE   Woof-woof.
              My doggie goes.... woof-woof.

MICHAEL   Whuuu-whuuu...

GABRIELLE   Woof-woof.

MICHAEL   Whew...

GABRIELLE   Oooof.

> *MICHAEL and GABRIELLE share a little laugh then they stop.*

MICHAEL   You... are good... for me...

GABRIELLE   *(beat)* Good night...

MICHAEL   ...sweet prince...

GABRIELLE   Angels...

MICHAEL   I know... I know...

> *GABRIELLE kisses his forehead.*

MICHAEL   *(smiling)* Ouch.

GABRIELLE   Ouch.

> *GABRIELLE leaves shuffling away as if looking for something.*
>
> *Lights fade.*

ACT TWO
Scene Ten

*Lights up on JOAN carrying a single rose.
She walks toward MICHAEL in the facility. He slumps in a chair or bed expression-
less but makes a terrible sucking noise
when he breathes. This happens throughout the scene.*

*JOAN puts the rose in a vase beside the
table, then watches MICHAEL breathe.
She goes to leave but has second thoughts
and returns to MICHAEL's side. She
wants to touch him.*

JOAN   Bastard.
I hate you.
I hate your jokes. I hate your constant
teasing. I hate your temper, your obses-
sion with unions, the Legion, the university and the NDP. I hate your barbeques,
your war stories, your war buddies and
your Buddy Holly record collection. I
hate your bird calls, your hiking trips and
your pipes, especially the one you bought
in Holland, the smell of tobacco, and how
you talk to cats. They're not human, you
know. I hate your shaving kit, your liquor
cabinet, your brown belt with the horse-
head silver buckle, your books and the
chess board you made when you were 12.
I really hate that. I hate the way you
crunched down Shreddies with cream
every morning at 7 a.m., and the way you
got me out of bed by blowing in my face,
the way you threw my covers off, the way
you pretended to listen to me, the way
you talked, the way you walked, your
hair, your face, your forehead, your eyes,
your mouth, and I really, really hate...

The sucking noise gets worse.

JOAN   Will you stop? Just stop it.

*JOAN takes a glass of water from beside
MICHAEL and gently tries to pour some
down his throat. He chokes on it.*

I'm sorry. My fault. I poured too fast. It's
okay. You're going to be okay, dad. Take
it easy... breathe. That's it. You're going to
be just fine. Just fine...

*MICHAEL recovers and leans against her
breast.*

I'm right here, dad. It's me... Joan. I'm
here, I'm right here—

*MICHAEL suddenly slumps away from
her. He groans. His breathing slows.
JOAN doesn't know what to do, finally she
reaches over and pours a little water in her
hand. Then she dabs his forehead and eyes
with a few drops. A baptism of sorts.
Then JOAN listens to his breath by putting an ear to his mouth.*

*She waits as MICHAEL stops breathing.
He dies. JOAN takes a drink of water from
the glass, then she walks away.*

*For a moment, nothing happens... then, out
of the shadows, GABRIELLE, wearing a
colourful outfit appears.*

*She walks up and studies his face. She
realizes he's dead.*

*Music fades up. It's the same grand classi-
cal music MARY liked earlier.*

> GABRIELLE *loves this music. She gently pulls MICHAEL to his feet.*

GABRIELLE   Come.

> *They dance. In the background ROBYN appears.*
>
> *GABRIELLE escorts MICHAEL toward ROBYN as other actors, including LEO and MARY 2, appear in the background, drifting out like moths attracted to light.*

GABRIELLE   *(to MICHAEL)* Right... right... good-bye, Michael.

> *MICHAEL finally walks toward ROBYN. She takes his hand and then they disappear into the dark.*
>
> *GABRIELLE leaves, slowly shuffling. A moment.*

LEO   What a night for a double header.

MARY 2   A warm evening is perfect for a slow dance.

LEO   (beat) Do you think they'll come for us?

MARY 2   Oh yes. I can feel it in my bones.

LEO   The bones are always the last to go.

MARY 2   That's why I brought our coats. Here.

> *MARY 2 and LEO help each other with their plain-looking overcoats, slowly putting them on over their colourful clothes. They look out toward the audience hopefully waiting.*

MARY 2   When they come, I'll be ready now.

LEO   Me too.

> *A blue sky appears behind them.*

> *LEO and MARY 2 reach out and hold hands.*

> *Lights fade.*

> THE END.

OTHER TITLES
BY
AARON BUSHKOWSKY

Dancing Backwards
An independent and successful businesswoman is
suddenly struck by Alzheimer's disease, and her
daughter and son-in-law struggle to cope.
2 acts   2m/2f
PUC (cs)   1-55155-128-4 $ 7.00

Java Life
Five people find hope, friendship, and cappuccino in
an all-night coffee bar.
2 acts   3m/2f
PUC (cs)   1-55173-529-6 (1998) $ 9.00

The Big Blue Bird
Three generations of men – grandfather, father, and
son – come to terms with the missing women in their
lives and find love and compassion.
1 act   3m
PUC (cs)   1-55290-050-9 (1999) $ 7.00

Available from Playwrights Union of Canada
416-703-0201   fax 703-0059
orders@puc.ca   http://www.puc.ca